I0084917

♠ *This Book Belongs To* ♠

_____

90 DAYS

CONNECTING WITH
GOD

By Becky Brooks

A Bible Study Journal
to Help You Better
Connect With God

90 Days Connecting With God
by Becky Brooks

Published by
Cross Point Publishing
Menomonie, Wisconsin 54751
www.crosspointpublishing.com

ALL RIGHTS RESERVED
No portion of this publication may be reproduced, stored in any electronic system or transmitted in any form or by any means, electronic, mechanical, photocopy, recording or otherwise, without the written permissions from the author and publisher. Brief quotations may be used in literary reviews

Unless otherwise indicated, all Scripture quotations are from The Holy Bible, English Standard Version ® (ESV®), copyright© 2011 by Crossway, a publishing ministry of Good News Publishers. Used by permission. All rights reserved

Scripture quotations marked (NIV) are taken from the Holy Bible, New International Version®, NIV®. Copyright © 1973, 1978, 1984, 2011 by Biblica, Inc ™ Used by permission of Zondervan. All rights reserved worldwide.

Scripture quotations marked (NLT) are taken from the Holy Bible, New Living Translation, copyright © 1996, 2004, 2007 by Tyndale House Foundation. Used by permission of Tyndale House Publishers, INC., Carol Stream, Illinois 60188. All Rights Reserved

Scripture quotations marked (KJV) are taken from the Holy Bible, King James Version. The KJV is public domain in the United States.

Copyright © 2013
by Becky Brooks
All Rights Reserved

ISBN-10: 0615769748
ISBN-13: 978-0615769745
Cross Point Publishing

Cover Design by: Jason M. Brooks
Cover photo courtesy of: www.morguefile.com

Find us on Facebook at:
www.facebook.com/CrossPointPublishing

Follow us on Twitter at:
@xpointpub

Cross Point offers great prices on bulk orders of our books. Contact our sales team to learn more. sales@crosspointpublishing.com

Check Out These Other Journal's From Becky Brooks

90 Days Walking With God
A Journal to Keep Track of Your Daily Food, Exercise, Thoughts and Prayers

ISBN: 978-0615740812

90 Days Praying With God
A Journal to Capture Your Next 90 Days of Prayer

ISBN: 978-0615744063

✝

*Pay attention to what
I say;
turn your ear to my words.
Do not let them out
of your sight,
keep them within
your heart;
for they are life
to those
who find them
and health to
one's whole body.
Above all else, guard
your heart,
for everything you do
flows from it.*

Proverbs 4: 20-23

✝

I have put together this 90 Day Bible Study Journal to help you while you travel through your bible, connecting with the words of our Lord.

Our Father has made it clear through the words of the bible, how important it is to know Him. I pray that you find this both helpful and useful in your journey these next 90 days. I hope that through this you will not only know Him better but feel a wonderful connection with Him.

Your Sister in Christ,
Becky Brooks

It is written,
"Man should not live on bread alone, but by every word that comes from the mouth of God."
Matthew 4:4

✝

I have put together this 90 Day Bible Study Journal to help you while you travel through your bible, connecting with the words of our Lord.

Our Father has made it clear through the words of the bible, how important it is to know Him. I pray that you find this both helpful and useful in your journey these next 90 days. I hope that through this you will not only know Him better but feel a wonderful connection with Him.

Your Sister in Christ,
Becky Brooks

It is written,
"Man should not live on bread alone, but by every word that comes from the mouth of God."
Matthew 4:4

Three Common Ways
To
Study Your Bible

Word Study

This is where you think of a word that interests you. Then research that word to get a deeper understanding of what it means in the bible and how & why it was used.

Topical Study

This is where you think of a topic of interest to you, such as forgiveness. You then focus your studying in that particular area.

Book Study

This is where you pick one of the books in the bible and dig right in. Reading the whole book, taking your time as you go. Please remember when doing a book study it is not about how far you read that day, it's about how much you got out of it. In this case, slower is better.

I would like you to remember these are only ideas, you may study your bible anyway that is best for you.

**Your word is a lamp to my feet
and a light to my path.**
Psalm 119:105

Five Other Helpful Hints

1. **Read The Bible Aloud**
   - If you find your mind drifting and you are starting to think of other things, try reading your bible out loud.

2. **Switch Bible Translations**
   - If you find the translation you are reading confusing, head to your local book store and check out different translations. (Some are easier to read than others)

3. **Listen To The Bible**
   - If you don't want to read your bible, just listen to it. You can find it on tape, cd, even on your electronic tablet.

4. **Schedule Time**
   - To make sure your day doesn't get away from you, put time aside on your schedule everyday just for your bible study.

5. **Mark Up Your Bible**
   - Don't be afraid to write, underline or even highlight in your bible.

You are now ready to begin!

Dear Lord, please allow the Holy Spirit to open my eyes and heart today as I read your word, so I can see the truth which it holds for me.   Amen

Day One

Date	Time	Place of Study

Please fill in which one applies to you today

Word Study	Topical Study	Book Study

What is God teaching you through these verses?

What are the key points you have learned through your study today?

Why do you think those specific words where chosen?

Is there anyone you should share what you've learned today with & why?

Extra notes:

Close your study today with a prayer

> Dear Lord, please allow the Holy Spirit to open my eyes and heart today as I read your word, so I can see the truth which it holds for me.   Amen

Day Two

Date	Time	Place of Study

Please fill in which one applies to you today

Word Study	Topical Study	Book Study

What is God teaching you through these verses?

What are the key points you have learned through your study today?

Why do you think those specific words where chosen?

Is there anyone you should share what you've learned today with & why?

Extra notes:

Close your study today with a prayer

Dear Lord, please allow the Holy Spirit to open my eyes and heart today as I read your word, so I can see the truth which it holds for me.   Amen

Day Three

Date	Time	Place of Study

Please fill in which one applies to you today

Word Study	Topical Study	Book Study

What is God teaching you through these verses?

What are the key points you have learned through your study today?

Why do you think those specific words where chosen?

Is there anyone you should share what you've learned today with & why?

Extra notes:

Close your study today with a prayer

> Dear Lord, please allow the Holy Spirit to open my eyes and heart today as I read your word, so I can see the truth which it holds for me.   Amen

Day Four

Date	Time	Place of Study

Please fill in which one applies to you today

Word Study	Topical Study	Book Study

What is God teaching you through these verses?

What are the key points you have learned through your study today?

Why do you think those specific words where chosen?

| |
| |
| |
| |
| |

Is there anyone you should share what you've learned today with & why?

| |
| |

Extra notes:

| |
| |
| |
| |
| |
| |
| |

Close your study today with a prayer

| |
| |
| |
| |
| |

> Dear Lord, please allow the Holy Spirit to open my eyes and heart today as I read your word, so I can see the truth which it holds for me.   Amen

Day Five

Date	Time	Place of Study

Please fill in which one applies to you today

Word Study	Topical Study	Book Study

What is God teaching you through these verses?

What are the key points you have learned through your study today?

Why do you think those specific words where chosen?

Is there anyone you should share what you've learned today with & why?

Extra notes:

Close your study today with a prayer

Dear Lord, please allow the Holy Spirit to open my eyes and heart today as I read your word, so I can see the truth which it holds for me.   Amen

Day Six

Date	Time	Place of Study

Please fill in which one applies to you today

Word Study	Topical Study	Book Study

What is God teaching you through these verses?

What are the key points you have learned through your study today?

Why do you think those specific words where chosen?

Is there anyone you should share what you've learned today with & why?

Extra notes:

Close your study today with a prayer

Dear Lord, please allow the Holy Spirit to open my eyes and heart today as I read your word, so I can see the truth which it holds for me.   Amen

Day Seven

Date	Time	Place of Study

Please fill in which one applies to you today

Word Study	Topical Study	Book Study

What is God teaching you through these verses?

What are the key points you have learned through your study today?

Why do you think those specific words where chosen?

Is there anyone you should share what you've learned today with & why?

Extra notes:

Close your study today with a prayer

Dear Lord, please allow the Holy Spirit to open my eyes and heart today as I read your word, so I can see the truth which it holds for me.   Amen

Day Eight

Date	Time	Place of Study

Please fill in which one applies to you today

Word Study	Topical Study	Book Study

What is God teaching you through these verses?

What are the key points you have learned through your study today?

Why do you think those specific words where chosen?

Is there anyone you should share what you've learned today with & why?

Extra notes:

Close your study today with a prayer

Dear Lord, please allow the Holy Spirit to open my eyes and heart today as I read your word, so I can see the truth which it holds for me.   Amen

Day Nine

Date	Time	Place of Study

Please fill in which one applies to you today

Word Study	Topical Study	Book Study

What is God teaching you through these verses?

What are the key points you have learned through your study today?

Why do you think those specific words where chosen?

Is there anyone you should share what you've learned today with & why?

Extra notes:

Close your study today with a prayer

> Dear Lord, please allow the Holy Spirit to open my eyes and heart today as I read your word, so I can see the truth which it holds for me.   Amen

Day Ten

Date	Time	Place of Study

Please fill in which one applies to you today

Word Study	Topical Study	Book Study

What is God teaching you through these verses?

What are the key points you have learned through your study today?

Why do you think those specific words where chosen?

Is there anyone you should share what you've learned today with & why?

Extra notes:

Close your study today with a prayer

Dear Lord, please allow the Holy Spirit to open my eyes and heart today as I read your word, so I can see the truth which it holds for me.   Amen

Day Eleven

Date	Time	Place of Study

Please fill in which one applies to you today

Word Study	Topical Study	Book Study

What is God teaching you through these verses?

What are the key points you have learned through your study today?

Why do you think those specific words where chosen?

Is there anyone you should share what you've learned today with & why?

Extra notes:

Close your study today with a prayer

> Dear Lord, please allow the Holy Spirit to open my eyes and heart today as I read your word, so I can see the truth which it holds for me.   Amen

Day Twelve

Date	Time	Place of Study

Please fill in which one applies to you today

Word Study	Topical Study	Book Study

What is God teaching you through these verses?

What are the key points you have learned through your study today?

Why do you think those specific words where chosen?

Is there anyone you should share what you've learned today with & why?

Extra notes:

Close your study today with a prayer

> Dear Lord, please allow the Holy Spirit to open my eyes and heart today as I read your word, so I can see the truth which it holds for me.   Amen

Day Thirteen

Date	Time	Place of Study

Please fill in which one applies to you today

Word Study	Topical Study	Book Study

What is God teaching you through these verses?

What are the key points you have learned through your study today?

Why do you think those specific words where chosen?

Is there anyone you should share what you've learned today with & why?

Extra notes:

Close your study today with a prayer

> Dear Lord, please allow the Holy Spirit to open my eyes and heart today as I read your word, so I can see the truth which it holds for me.   Amen

Day Fourteen

Date	Time	Place of Study

Please fill in which one applies to you today

Word Study	Topical Study	Book Study

What is God teaching you through these verses?

What are the key points you have learned through your study today?

Why do you think those specific words where chosen?

Is there anyone you should share what you've learned today with & why?

Extra notes:

Close your study today with a prayer

Dear Lord, please allow the Holy Spirit to open my eyes and heart today as I read your word, so I can see the truth which it holds for me.   Amen

Day Fifteen

Date	Time	Place of Study

Please fill in which one applies to you today

Word Study	Topical Study	Book Study

What is God teaching you through these verses?

What are the key points you have learned through your study today?

Why do you think those specific words where chosen?

Is there anyone you should share what you've learned today with & why?

Extra notes:

Close your study today with a prayer

> Dear Lord, please allow the Holy Spirit to open my eyes and heart today as I read your word, so I can see the truth which it holds for me.   Amen

Day Sixteen

Date	Time	Place of Study

Please fill in which one applies to you today

Word Study	Topical Study	Book Study

What is God teaching you through these verses?

What are the key points you have learned through your study today?

Why do you think those specific words where chosen?

Is there anyone you should share what you've learned today with & why?

Extra notes:

Close your study today with a prayer

Dear Lord, please allow the Holy Spirit to open my eyes and heart today as I read your word, so I can see the truth which it holds for me. Amen

Day Seventeen

Date	Time	Place of Study

Please fill in which one applies to you today

Word Study	Topical Study	Book Study

What is God teaching you through these verses?

What are the key points you have learned through your study today?

Why do you think those specific words where chosen?

Is there anyone you should share what you've learned today with & why?

Extra notes:

Close your study today with a prayer

Dear Lord, please allow the Holy Spirit to open my eyes and heart today as I read your word, so I can see the truth which it holds for me.   Amen

Day Eighteen

Date	Time	Place of Study

Please fill in which one applies to you today

Word Study	Topical Study	Book Study

What is God teaching you through these verses?

What are the key points you have learned through your study today?

Why do you think those specific words where chosen?

Is there anyone you should share what you've learned today with & why?

Extra notes:

Close your study today with a prayer

Dear Lord, please allow the Holy Spirit to open my eyes and heart today as I read your word, so I can see the truth which it holds for me.   Amen

Day Nineteen

Date	Time	Place of Study

Please fill in which one applies to you today

Word Study	Topical Study	Book Study

What is God teaching you through these verses?

What are the key points you have learned through your study today?

Why do you think those specific words where chosen?

Is there anyone you should share what you've learned today with & why?

Extra notes:

Close your study today with a prayer

> Dear Lord, please allow the Holy Spirit to open my eyes and heart today as I read your word, so I can see the truth which it holds for me.   Amen

Day Twenty

Date	Time	Place of Study

Please fill in which one applies to you today

Word Study	Topical Study	Book Study

What is God teaching you through these verses?

What are the key points you have learned through your study today?

Why do you think those specific words where chosen?

Is there anyone you should share what you've learned today with & why?

Extra notes:

Close your study today with a prayer

Dear Lord, please allow the Holy Spirit to open my eyes and heart today as I read your word, so I can see the truth which it holds for me.   Amen

Day Twenty~One

Date	Time	Place of Study

Please fill in which one applies to you today

Word Study	Topical Study	Book Study

What is God teaching you through these verses?

What are the key points you have learned through your study today?

Why do you think those specific words where chosen?

Is there anyone you should share what you've learned today with & why?

Extra notes:

Close your study today with a prayer

Dear Lord, please allow the Holy Spirit to open my eyes and heart today as I read your word, so I can see the truth which it holds for me.   Amen

Day Twenty~Two

Date	Time	Place of Study

Please fill in which one applies to you today

Word Study	Topical Study	Book Study

What is God teaching you through these verses?

What are the key points you have learned through your study today?

Why do you think those specific words where chosen?

Is there anyone you should share what you've learned today with & why?

Extra notes:

Close your study today with a prayer

> Dear Lord, please allow the Holy Spirit to open my eyes and heart today as I read your word, so I can see the truth which it holds for me.   Amen

Day Twenty~Three

Date	Time	Place of Study

Please fill in which one applies to you today

Word Study	Topical Study	Book Study

What is God teaching you through these verses?

What are the key points you have learned through your study today?

Why do you think those specific words where chosen?

Is there anyone you should share what you've learned today with & why?

Extra notes:

Close your study today with a prayer

Dear Lord, please allow the Holy Spirit to open my eyes and heart today as I read your word, so I can see the truth which it holds for me.   Amen

Day Twenty~Four

Date	Time	Place of Study

Please fill in which one applies to you today

Word Study	Topical Study	Book Study

What is God teaching you through these verses?

What are the key points you have learned through your study today?

Why do you think those specific words where chosen?

Is there anyone you should share what you've learned today with & why?

Extra notes:

Close your study today with a prayer

Dear Lord, please allow the Holy Spirit to open my eyes and heart today as I read your word, so I can see the truth which it holds for me. Amen

Day Twenty~Five

Date	Time	Place of Study

Please fill in which one applies to you today

Word Study	Topical Study	Book Study

What is God teaching you through these verses?

What are the key points you have learned through your study today?

Why do you think those specific words where chosen?

Is there anyone you should share what you've learned today with & why?

Extra notes:

Close your study today with a prayer

Dear Lord, please allow the Holy Spirit to open my eyes and heart today as I read your word, so I can see the truth which it holds for me.   Amen

Day Twenty~Six

Date	Time	Place of Study

Please fill in which one applies to you today

Word Study	Topical Study	Book Study

What is God teaching you through these verses?

What are the key points you have learned through your study today?

Why do you think those specific words where chosen?

Is there anyone you should share what you've learned today with & why?

Extra notes:

Close your study today with a prayer

Dear Lord, please allow the Holy Spirit to open my eyes and heart today as I read your word, so I can see the truth which it holds for me.   Amen

Day Twenty~Seven

Date	Time	Place of Study

Please fill in which one applies to you today

Word Study	Topical Study	Book Study

What is God teaching you through these verses?

What are the key points you have learned through your study today?

Why do you think those specific words where chosen?

Is there anyone you should share what you've learned today with & why?

Extra notes:

Close your study today with a prayer

Dear Lord, please allow the Holy Spirit to open my eyes and heart today as I read your word, so I can see the truth which it holds for me.   Amen

Day Twenty~Eight

Date	Time	Place of Study

Please fill in which one applies to you today

Word Study	Topical Study	Book Study

What is God teaching you through these verses?

What are the key points you have learned through your study today?

Why do you think those specific words where chosen?

Is there anyone you should share what you've learned today with & why?

Extra notes:

Close your study today with a prayer

Dear Lord, please allow the Holy Spirit to open my eyes and heart today as I read your word, so I can see the truth which it holds for me.   Amen

Day Twenty~Nine

Date	Time	Place of Study

Please fill in which one applies to you today

Word Study	Topical Study	Book Study

What is God teaching you through these verses?

What are the key points you have learned through your study today?

Why do you think those specific words where chosen?

Is there anyone you should share what you've learned today with & why?

Extra notes:

Close your study today with a prayer

Dear Lord, please allow the Holy Spirit to open my eyes and heart today as I read your word, so I can see the truth which it holds for me.   Amen

Day Thirty

Date	Time	Place of Study

Please fill in which one applies to you today

Word Study	Topical Study	Book Study

What is God teaching you through these verses?

What are the key points you have learned through your study today?

Why do you think those specific words where chosen?

| |
| |
| |
| |
| |

Is there anyone you should share what you've learned today with & why?

| |
| |

Extra notes:

| |
| |
| |
| |
| |
| |
| |

Close your study today with a prayer

| |
| |
| |
| |
| |

Dear Lord, please allow the Holy Spirit to open my eyes and heart today as I read your word, so I can see the truth which it holds for me.   Amen

Day Thirty~One

Date	Time	Place of Study

Please fill in which one applies to you today

Word Study	Topical Study	Book Study

What is God teaching you through these verses?

What are the key points you have learned through your study today?

Why do you think those specific words where chosen?

Is there anyone you should share what you've learned today with & why?

Extra notes:

Close your study today with a prayer

> Dear Lord, please allow the Holy Spirit to open my eyes and heart today as I read your word, so I can see the truth which it holds for me.   Amen

Day Thirty~Two

Date	Time	Place of Study

Please fill in which one applies to you today

Word Study	Topical Study	Book Study

What is God teaching you through these verses?

What are the key points you have learned through your study today?

Why do you think those specific words where chosen?

Is there anyone you should share what you've learned today with & why?

Extra notes:

Close your study today with a prayer

Dear Lord, please allow the Holy Spirit to open my eyes and heart today as I read your word, so I can see the truth which it holds for me.   Amen

Day Thirty~Three

Date	Time	Place of Study

Please fill in which one applies to you today

Word Study	Topical Study	Book Study

What is God teaching you through these verses?

What are the key points you have learned through your study today?

Why do you think those specific words where chosen?

Is there anyone you should share what you've learned today with & why?

Extra notes:

Close your study today with a prayer

Dear Lord, please allow the Holy Spirit to open my eyes and heart today as I read your word, so I can see the truth which it holds for me.   Amen

Day Thirty~Four

Date	Time	Place of Study

Please fill in which one applies to you today

Word Study	Topical Study	Book Study

What is God teaching you through these verses?

What are the key points you have learned through your study today?

Why do you think those specific words where chosen?

Is there anyone you should share what you've learned today with & why?

Extra notes:

Close your study today with a prayer

> Dear Lord, please allow the Holy Spirit to open
> my eyes and heart today as I read your word, so
> I can see the truth which it holds for me.   Amen

Day Thirty~Five

Date	Time	Place of Study

Please fill in which one applies to you today

Word Study	Topical Study	Book Study

What is God teaching you through these verses?

What are the key points you have learned through your study today?

Why do you think those specific words where chosen?

Is there anyone you should share what you've learned today with & why?

Extra notes:

Close your study today with a prayer

Dear Lord, please allow the Holy Spirit to open my eyes and heart today as I read your word, so I can see the truth which it holds for me.   Amen

Day Thirty~Six

Date	Time	Place of Study

Please fill in which one applies to you today

Word Study	Topical Study	Book Study

What is God teaching you through these verses?

What are the key points you have learned through your study today?

Why do you think those specific words where chosen?

Is there anyone you should share what you've learned today with & why?

Extra notes:

Close your study today with a prayer

Dear Lord, please allow the Holy Spirit to open my eyes and heart today as I read your word, so I can see the truth which it holds for me.   Amen

Day Thirty~Seven

Date	Time	Place of Study

Please fill in which one applies to you today

Word Study	Topical Study	Book Study

What is God teaching you through these verses?

What are the key points you have learned through your study today?

Why do you think those specific words where chosen?

Is there anyone you should share what you've learned today with & why?

Extra notes:

Close your study today with a prayer

Dear Lord, please allow the Holy Spirit to open my eyes and heart today as I read your word, so I can see the truth which it holds for me.   Amen

Day Thirty~Eight

Date	Time	Place of Study

Please fill in which one applies to you today

Word Study	Topical Study	Book Study

What is God teaching you through these verses?

What are the key points you have learned through your study today?

Why do you think those specific words where chosen?

Is there anyone you should share what you've learned today with & why?

Extra notes:

Close your study today with a prayer

Dear Lord, please allow the Holy Spirit to open my eyes and heart today as I read your word, so I can see the truth which it holds for me. Amen

Day Thirty~Nine

Date	Time	Place of Study

Please fill in which one applies to you today

Word Study	Topical Study	Book Study

What is God teaching you through these verses?

What are the key points you have learned through your study today?

Why do you think those specific words where chosen?

Is there anyone you should share what you've learned today with & why?

Extra notes:

Close your study today with a prayer

Dear Lord, please allow the Holy Spirit to open my eyes and heart today as I read your word, so I can see the truth which it holds for me.   Amen

Day Forty

Date	Time	Place of Study

Please fill in which one applies to you today

Word Study	Topical Study	Book Study

What is God teaching you through these verses?

What are the key points you have learned through your study today?

Why do you think those specific words where chosen?

Is there anyone you should share what you've learned today with & why?

Extra notes:

Close your study today with a prayer

Dear Lord, please allow the Holy Spirit to open my eyes and heart today as I read your word, so I can see the truth which it holds for me.   Amen

Day Forty~One

Date	Time	Place of Study

Please fill in which one applies to you today

Word Study	Topical Study	Book Study

What is God teaching you through these verses?

What are the key points you have learned through your study today?

Why do you think those specific words where chosen?

Is there anyone you should share what you've learned today with & why?

Extra notes:

Close your study today with a prayer

Dear Lord, please allow the Holy Spirit to open my eyes and heart today as I read your word, so I can see the truth which it holds for me.   Amen

Day Forty~Two

Date	Time	Place of Study

Please fill in which one applies to you today

Word Study	Topical Study	Book Study

What is God teaching you through these verses?

What are the key points you have learned through your study today?

Why do you think those specific words where chosen?

Is there anyone you should share what you've learned today with & why?

Extra notes:

Close your study today with a prayer

Dear Lord, please allow the Holy Spirit to open my eyes and heart today as I read your word, so I can see the truth which it holds for me.   Amen

Day Forty~Three

Date	Time	Place of Study

Please fill in which one applies to you today

Word Study	Topical Study	Book Study

What is God teaching you through these verses?

What are the key points you have learned through your study today?

Why do you think those specific words where chosen?

Is there anyone you should share what you've learned today with & why?

Extra notes:

Close your study today with a prayer

> Dear Lord, please allow the Holy Spirit to open my eyes and heart today as I read your word, so I can see the truth which it holds for me.   Amen

Day Forty~Four

Date	Time	Place of Study

Please fill in which one applies to you today

Word Study	Topical Study	Book Study

What is God teaching you through these verses?

What are the key points you have learned through your study today?

Why do you think those specific words where chosen?

Is there anyone you should share what you've learned today with & why?

Extra notes:

Close your study today with a prayer

> Dear Lord, please allow the Holy Spirit to open my eyes and heart today as I read your word, so I can see the truth which it holds for me.   Amen

Day Forty~Five

Date	Time	Place of Study

Please fill in which one applies to you today

Word Study	Topical Study	Book Study

What is God teaching you through these verses?

What are the key points you have learned through your study today?

Why do you think those specific words where chosen?

Is there anyone you should share what you've learned today with & why?

Extra notes:

Close your study today with a prayer

Dear Lord, please allow the Holy Spirit to open my eyes and heart today as I read your word, so I can see the truth which it holds for me.   Amen

Day Forty~Six

Date	Time	Place of Study

Please fill in which one applies to you today

Word Study	Topical Study	Book Study

What is God teaching you through these verses?

What are the key points you have learned through your study today?

Why do you think those specific words where chosen?

Is there anyone you should share what you've learned today with & why?

Extra notes:

Close your study today with a prayer

Dear Lord, please allow the Holy Spirit to open
my eyes and heart today as I read your word, so
I can see the truth which it holds for me.   Amen

Day Forty~Seven

Date	Time	Place of Study

Please fill in which one applies to you today

Word Study	Topical Study	Book Study

What is God teaching you through these verses?

What are the key points you have learned through your study today?

Why do you think those specific words where chosen?

Is there anyone you should share what you've learned today with & why?

Extra notes:

Close your study today with a prayer

Dear Lord, please allow the Holy Spirit to open my eyes and heart today as I read your word, so I can see the truth which it holds for me.   Amen

Day Forty~Eight

Date	Time	Place of Study

Please fill in which one applies to you today

Word Study	Topical Study	Book Study

What is God teaching you through these verses?

What are the key points you have learned through your study today?

Why do you think those specific words where chosen?

Is there anyone you should share what you've learned today with & why?

Extra notes:

Close your study today with a prayer

Dear Lord, please allow the Holy Spirit to open my eyes and heart today as I read your word, so I can see the truth which it holds for me.   Amen

Day Forty~Nine

Date	Time	Place of Study

Please fill in which one applies to you today

Word Study	Topical Study	Book Study

What is God teaching you through these verses?

What are the key points you have learned through your study today?

Why do you think those specific words where chosen?

Is there anyone you should share what you've learned today with & why?

Extra notes:

Close your study today with a prayer

> Dear Lord, please allow the Holy Spirit to open my eyes and heart today as I read your word, so I can see the truth which it holds for me.   Amen

Day Fifty

Date	Time	Place of Study

Please fill in which one applies to you today

Word Study	Topical Study	Book Study

What is God teaching you through these verses?

What are the key points you have learned through your study today?

Why do you think those specific words where chosen?

Is there anyone you should share what you've learned today with & why?

Extra notes:

Close your study today with a prayer

Dear Lord, please allow the Holy Spirit to open my eyes and heart today as I read your word, so I can see the truth which it holds for me.   Amen

Day Fifty~One

Date	Time	Place of Study

Please fill in which one applies to you today

Word Study	Topical Study	Book Study

What is God teaching you through these verses?

What are the key points you have learned through your study today?

Why do you think those specific words where chosen?

Is there anyone you should share what you've learned today with & why?

Extra notes:

Close your study today with a prayer

Dear Lord, please allow the Holy Spirit to open my eyes and heart today as I read your word, so I can see the truth which it holds for me.   Amen

Day Fifty~Two

Date	Time	Place of Study

Please fill in which one applies to you today

Word Study	Topical Study	Book Study

What is God teaching you through these verses?

What are the key points you have learned through your study today?

Why do you think those specific words where chosen?

Is there anyone you should share what you've learned today with & why?

Extra notes:

Close your study today with a prayer

Dear Lord, please allow the Holy Spirit to open my eyes and heart today as I read your word, so I can see the truth which it holds for me.   Amen

Day Fifty-Three

Date	Time	Place of Study

Please fill in which one applies to you today

Word Study	Topical Study	Book Study

What is God teaching you through these verses?

What are the key points you have learned through your study today?

Why do you think those specific words where chosen?

Is there anyone you should share what you've learned today with & why?

Extra notes:

Close your study today with a prayer

Dear Lord, please allow the Holy Spirit to open my eyes and heart today as I read your word, so I can see the truth which it holds for me.   Amen

Day Fifty~Four

Date	Time	Place of Study

Please fill in which one applies to you today

Word Study	Topical Study	Book Study

What is God teaching you through these verses?

What are the key points you have learned through your study today?

Why do you think those specific words where chosen?

Is there anyone you should share what you've learned today with & why?

Extra notes:

Close your study today with a prayer

Dear Lord, please allow the Holy Spirit to open my eyes and heart today as I read your word, so I can see the truth which it holds for me.   Amen

Day Fifty~Five

Date	Time	Place of Study

Please fill in which one applies to you today

Word Study	Topical Study	Book Study

What is God teaching you through these verses?

What are the key points you have learned through your study today?

Why do you think those specific words where chosen?

Is there anyone you should share what you've learned today with & why?

Extra notes:

Close your study today with a prayer

Dear Lord, please allow the Holy Spirit to open my eyes and heart today as I read your word, so I can see the truth which it holds for me.   Amen

Day Fifty~Six

Date	Time	Place of Study

Please fill in which one applies to you today

Word Study	Topical Study	Book Study

What is God teaching you through these verses?

What are the key points you have learned through your study today?

Why do you think those specific words where chosen?

Is there anyone you should share what you've learned today with & why?

Extra notes:

Close your study today with a prayer

Dear Lord, please allow the Holy Spirit to open my eyes and heart today as I read your word, so I can see the truth which it holds for me.   Amen

Day Fifty~Seven

Date	Time	Place of Study

Please fill in which one applies to you today

Word Study	Topical Study	Book Study

What is God teaching you through these verses?

What are the key points you have learned through your study today?

Why do you think those specific words where chosen?

Is there anyone you should share what you've learned today with & why?

Extra notes:

Close your study today with a prayer

Dear Lord, please allow the Holy Spirit to open my eyes and heart today as I read your word, so I can see the truth which it holds for me.   Amen

Day Fifty~Eight

Date	Time	Place of Study

Please fill in which one applies to you today

Word Study	Topical Study	Book Study

What is God teaching you through these verses?

What are the key points you have learned through your study today?

Why do you think those specific words where chosen?

Is there anyone you should share what you've learned today with & why?

Extra notes:

Close your study today with a prayer

Dear Lord, please allow the Holy Spirit to open my eyes and heart today as I read your word, so I can see the truth which it holds for me.   Amen

Day Fifty~Nine

Date	Time	Place of Study

Please fill in which one applies to you today

Word Study	Topical Study	Book Study

What is God teaching you through these verses?

What are the key points you have learned through your study today?

Why do you think those specific words where chosen?

Is there anyone you should share what you've learned today with & why?

Extra notes:

Close your study today with a prayer

Dear Lord, please allow the Holy Spirit to open my eyes and heart today as I read your word, so I can see the truth which it holds for me.   Amen

Day Sixty

Date	Time	Place of Study

Please fill in which one applies to you today

Word Study	Topical Study	Book Study

What is God teaching you through these verses?

What are the key points you have learned through your study today?

Why do you think those specific words where chosen?

Is there anyone you should share what you've learned today with & why?

Extra notes:

Close your study today with a prayer

Dear Lord, please allow the Holy Spirit to open my eyes and heart today as I read your word, so I can see the truth which it holds for me.   Amen

Day Sixty~One

Date	Time	Place of Study

Please fill in which one applies to you today

Word Study	Topical Study	Book Study

What is God teaching you through these verses?

What are the key points you have learned through your study today?

Why do you think those specific words where chosen?

Is there anyone you should share what you've learned today with & why?

Extra notes:

Close your study today with a prayer

Dear Lord, please allow the Holy Spirit to open my eyes and heart today as I read your word, so I can see the truth which it holds for me.   Amen

Day Sixty~Two

Date	Time	Place of Study

Please fill in which one applies to you today

Word Study	Topical Study	Book Study

What is God teaching you through these verses?

What are the key points you have learned through your study today?

Why do you think those specific words where chosen?

Is there anyone you should share what you've learned today with & why?

Extra notes:

Close your study today with a prayer

Dear Lord, please allow the Holy Spirit to open my eyes and heart today as I read your word, so I can see the truth which it holds for me.   Amen

Day Sixty~Three

Date	Time	Place of Study

Please fill in which one applies to you today

Word Study	Topical Study	Book Study

What is God teaching you through these verses?

What are the key points you have learned through your study today?

Why do you think those specific words where chosen?

Is there anyone you should share what you've learned today with & why?

Extra notes:

Close your study today with a prayer

Dear Lord, please allow the Holy Spirit to open my eyes and heart today as I read your word, so I can see the truth which it holds for me.   Amen

Day Sixty~Four

Date	Time	Place of Study

Please fill in which one applies to you today

Word Study	Topical Study	Book Study

What is God teaching you through these verses?

What are the key points you have learned through your study today?

Why do you think those specific words where chosen?

Is there anyone you should share what you've learned today with & why?

Extra notes:

Close your study today with a prayer

Dear Lord, please allow the Holy Spirit to open my eyes and heart today as I read your word, so I can see the truth which it holds for me.   Amen

Day Sixty~Five

Date	Time	Place of Study

Please fill in which one applies to you today

Word Study	Topical Study	Book Study

What is God teaching you through these verses?

What are the key points you have learned through your study today?

Why do you think those specific words where chosen?

Is there anyone you should share what you've learned today with & why?

Extra notes:

Close your study today with a prayer

Dear Lord, please allow the Holy Spirit to open my eyes and heart today as I read your word, so I can see the truth which it holds for me. Amen

Day Sixty~Six

Date	Time	Place of Study

Please fill in which one applies to you today

Word Study	Topical Study	Book Study

What is God teaching you through these verses?

What are the key points you have learned through your study today?

Why do you think those specific words where chosen?

Is there anyone you should share what you've learned today with & why?

Extra notes:

Close your study today with a prayer

Dear Lord, please allow the Holy Spirit to open my eyes and heart today as I read your word, so I can see the truth which it holds for me.   Amen

Day Sixty~Seven

Date	Time	Place of Study

Please fill in which one applies to you today

Word Study	Topical Study	Book Study

What is God teaching you through these verses?

What are the key points you have learned through your study today?

Why do you think those specific words where chosen?

Is there anyone you should share what you've learned today with & why?

Extra notes:

Close your study today with a prayer

Dear Lord, please allow the Holy Spirit to open my eyes and heart today as I read your word, so I can see the truth which it holds for me.   Amen

Day Sixty~Eight

Date	Time	Place of Study

Please fill in which one applies to you today

Word Study	Topical Study	Book Study

What is God teaching you through these verses?

What are the key points you have learned through your study today?

Why do you think those specific words where chosen?

Is there anyone you should share what you've learned today with & why?

Extra notes:

Close your study today with a prayer

Dear Lord, please allow the Holy Spirit to open my eyes and heart today as I read your word, so I can see the truth which it holds for me.   Amen

Day Sixty~Nine

Date	Time	Place of Study

Please fill in which one applies to you today

Word Study	Topical Study	Book Study

What is God teaching you through these verses?

What are the key points you have learned through your study today?

Why do you think those specific words where chosen?

Is there anyone you should share what you've learned today with & why?

Extra notes:

Close your study today with a prayer

Dear Lord, please allow the Holy Spirit to open my eyes and heart today as I read your word, so I can see the truth which it holds for me.   Amen

Day Seventy

Date	Time	Place of Study

Please fill in which one applies to you today

Word Study	Topical Study	Book Study

What is God teaching you through these verses?

What are the key points you have learned through your study today?

Why do you think those specific words where chosen?

Is there anyone you should share what you've learned today with & why?

Extra notes:

Close your study today with a prayer

Dear Lord, please allow the Holy Spirit to open my eyes and heart today as I read your word, so I can see the truth which it holds for me.   Amen

Day Seventy~One

Date	Time	Place of Study

Please fill in which one applies to you today

Word Study	Topical Study	Book Study

What is God teaching you through these verses?

What are the key points you have learned through your study today?

Why do you think those specific words where chosen?

Is there anyone you should share what you've learned today with & why?

Extra notes:

Close your study today with a prayer

Dear Lord, please allow the Holy Spirit to open my eyes and heart today as I read your word, so I can see the truth which it holds for me. Amen

Day Seventy~Two

Date	Time	Place of Study

Please fill in which one applies to you today

Word Study	Topical Study	Book Study

What is God teaching you through these verses?

What are the key points you have learned through your study today?

Why do you think those specific words where chosen?

Is there anyone you should share what you've learned today with & why?

Extra notes:

Close your study today with a prayer

Dear Lord, please allow the Holy Spirit to open my eyes and heart today as I read your word, so I can see the truth which it holds for me.   Amen

Day Seventy~Three

Date	Time	Place of Study

Please fill in which one applies to you today

Word Study	Topical Study	Book Study

What is God teaching you through these verses?

What are the key points you have learned through your study today?

Why do you think those specific words where chosen?

Is there anyone you should share what you've learned today with & why?

Extra notes:

Close your study today with a prayer

Dear Lord, please allow the Holy Spirit to open my eyes and heart today as I read your word, so I can see the truth which it holds for me.   Amen

Day Seventy~Four

Date	Time	Place of Study

Please fill in which one applies to you today

Word Study	Topical Study	Book Study

What is God teaching you through these verses?

What are the key points you have learned through your study today?

Why do you think those specific words where chosen?

Is there anyone you should share what you've learned today with & why?

Extra notes:

Close your study today with a prayer

Dear Lord, please allow the Holy Spirit to open my eyes and heart today as I read your word, so I can see the truth which it holds for me. Amen

Day Seventy~Five

Date	Time	Place of Study

Please fill in which one applies to you today

Word Study	Topical Study	Book Study

What is God teaching you through these verses?

What are the key points you have learned through your study today?

Why do you think those specific words where chosen?

Is there anyone you should share what you've learned today with & why?

Extra notes:

Close your study today with a prayer

> Dear Lord, please allow the Holy Spirit to open my eyes and heart today as I read your word, so I can see the truth which it holds for me.   Amen

Day Seventy~Six

Date	Time	Place of Study

Please fill in which one applies to you today

Word Study	Topical Study	Book Study

What is God teaching you through these verses?

What are the key points you have learned through your study today?

Why do you think those specific words where chosen?

Is there anyone you should share what you've learned today with & why?

Extra notes:

Close your study today with a prayer

Dear Lord, please allow the Holy Spirit to open my eyes and heart today as I read your word, so I can see the truth which it holds for me. Amen

Day Seventy~Seven

Date	Time	Place of Study

Please fill in which one applies to you today

Word Study	Topical Study	Book Study

What is God teaching you through these verses?

What are the key points you have learned through your study today?

Why do you think those specific words where chosen?

Is there anyone you should share what you've learned today with & why?

Extra notes:

Close your study today with a prayer

> Dear Lord, please allow the Holy Spirit to open my eyes and heart today as I read your word, so I can see the truth which it holds for me.   Amen

Day Seventy~Eight

Date	Time	Place of Study

Please fill in which one applies to you today

Word Study	Topical Study	Book Study

What is God teaching you through these verses?

What are the key points you have learned through your study today?

Why do you think those specific words where chosen?

Is there anyone you should share what you've learned today with & why?

Extra notes:

Close your study today with a prayer

Dear Lord, please allow the Holy Spirit to open my eyes and heart today as I read your word, so I can see the truth which it holds for me.   Amen

Day Seventy~Nine

Date	Time	Place of Study

Please fill in which one applies to you today

Word Study	Topical Study	Book Study

What is God teaching you through these verses?

What are the key points you have learned through your study today?

Why do you think those specific words where chosen?

Is there anyone you should share what you've learned today with & why?

Extra notes:

Close your study today with a prayer

Dear Lord, please allow the Holy Spirit to open my eyes and heart today as I read your word, so I can see the truth which it holds for me.   Amen

Day Eighty

Date	Time	Place of Study

Please fill in which one applies to you today

Word Study	Topical Study	Book Study

What is God teaching you through these verses?

What are the key points you have learned through your study today?

Why do you think those specific words where chosen?

Is there anyone you should share what you've learned today with & why?

Extra notes:

Close your study today with a prayer

Dear Lord, please allow the Holy Spirit to open my eyes and heart today as I read your word, so I can see the truth which it holds for me.   Amen

Day Eighty~One

Date	Time	Place of Study

Please fill in which one applies to you today

Word Study	Topical Study	Book Study

What is God teaching you through these verses?

What are the key points you have learned through your study today?

Why do you think those specific words where chosen?

Is there anyone you should share what you've learned today with & why?

Extra notes:

Close your study today with a prayer

Dear Lord, please allow the Holy Spirit to open my eyes and heart today as I read your word, so I can see the truth which it holds for me.   Amen

Day Eighty~Two

Date	Time	Place of Study

Please fill in which one applies to you today

Word Study	Topical Study	Book Study

What is God teaching you through these verses?

What are the key points you have learned through your study today?

Why do you think those specific words where chosen?

Is there anyone you should share what you've learned today with & why?

Extra notes:

Close your study today with a prayer

Dear Lord, please allow the Holy Spirit to open my eyes and heart today as I read your word, so I can see the truth which it holds for me.   Amen

Day Eighty~Three

Date	Time	Place of Study

Please fill in which one applies to you today

Word Study	Topical Study	Book Study

What is God teaching you through these verses?

What are the key points you have learned through your study today?

Why do you think those specific words where chosen?

Is there anyone you should share what you've learned today with & why?

Extra notes:

Close your study today with a prayer

Dear Lord, please allow the Holy Spirit to open my eyes and heart today as I read your word, so I can see the truth which it holds for me.   Amen

Day Eighty~Four

Date	Time	Place of Study

Please fill in which one applies to you today

Word Study	Topical Study	Book Study

What is God teaching you through these verses?

What are the key points you have learned through your study today?

Why do you think those specific words where chosen?

Is there anyone you should share what you've learned today with & why?

Extra notes:

Close your study today with a prayer

> Dear Lord, please allow the Holy Spirit to open my eyes and heart today as I read your word, so I can see the truth which it holds for me.   Amen

Day Eighty~Five

Date	Time	Place of Study

Please fill in which one applies to you today

Word Study	Topical Study	Book Study

What is God teaching you through these verses?

What are the key points you have learned through your study today?

Why do you think those specific words where chosen?

Is there anyone you should share what you've learned today with & why?

Extra notes:

Close your study today with a prayer

Dear Lord, please allow the Holy Spirit to open my eyes and heart today as I read your word, so I can see the truth which it holds for me.   Amen

Day Eighty~Six

Date	Time	Place of Study

Please fill in which one applies to you today

Word Study	Topical Study	Book Study

What is God teaching you through these verses?

What are the key points you have learned through your study today?

Why do you think those specific words where chosen?

Is there anyone you should share what you've learned today with & why?

Extra notes:

Close your study today with a prayer

Dear Lord, please allow the Holy Spirit to open my eyes and heart today as I read your word, so I can see the truth which it holds for me.   Amen

Day Eighty~Seventy

Date	Time	Place of Study

Please fill in which one applies to you today

Word Study	Topical Study	Book Study

What is God teaching you through these verses?

What are the key points you have learned through your study today?

Why do you think those specific words where chosen?

Is there anyone you should share what you've learned today with & why?

Extra notes:

Close your study today with a prayer

Dear Lord, please allow the Holy Spirit to open my eyes and heart today as I read your word, so I can see the truth which it holds for me. Amen

Day Eighty~Eight

Date	Time	Place of Study

Please fill in which one applies to you today

Word Study	Topical Study	Book Study

What is God teaching you through these verses?

What are the key points you have learned through your study today?

Why do you think those specific words where chosen?

Is there anyone you should share what you've learned today with & why?

Extra notes:

Close your study today with a prayer

Dear Lord, please allow the Holy Spirit to open my eyes and heart today as I read your word, so I can see the truth which it holds for me.   Amen

Day Eighty~Nine

Date	Time	Place of Study

Please fill in which one applies to you today

Word Study	Topical Study	Book Study

What is God teaching you through these verses?

What are the key points you have learned through your study today?

Why do you think those specific words where chosen?

Is there anyone you should share what you've learned today with & why?

Extra notes:

Close your study today with a prayer

> Dear Lord, please allow the Holy Spirit to open my eyes and heart today as I read your word, so I can see the truth which it holds for me.   Amen

Day Ninety

Date	Time	Place of Study

Please fill in which one applies to you today

Word Study	Topical Study	Book Study

What is God teaching you through these verses?

What are the key points you have learned through your study today?

Why do you think those specific words where chosen?

Is there anyone you should share what you've learned today with & why?

Extra notes:

Close your study today with a prayer

Dear Sister,

I hope you can now take some time and read over your studies, and see how the Lord has been revealing Himself to you.

Don't stop here. I urge you to continue with your bible studies. Studying our Lord's word daily is something He desires for us.

Please remember that the Lord will ALWAYS be there for you and that you can find great comfort in His word!

I am so proud of you for going on this 90 day bible study journey,

Becky Brooks

Keep In Touch With Me At My Website:
www.beckybrooks.net

Enjoy These Other Great Journal's From Becky Brooks!

90 DAYS WALKING WITH GOD

90 DAYS WALKING WITH GOD
By Becky Brooks

A Journal to Keep Track of Your Daily Food, Exercise, Thoughts and Prayers

90 DAYS CONNECTING WITH GOD
By Becky Brooks

A Bible Study Journal to Help You Better Connect With God

90 DAYS PRAYING WITH GOD
By Becky Brooks

A Journal to Capture Your Next 90 Days of Prayer

Take A Look At:
www.crosspointpublishing.com

Cross Point Publishing

www.ingramcontent.com/pod-product-compliance
Lightning Source LLC
Chambersburg PA
CBHW060923040426
42445CB00011B/765

* 9 7 8 0 6 1 5 7 6 9 7 4 5 *